Palo Alto City Library

Raising Cows on the Koebels' Farm

written by
ALICE K. FLANAGAN

photographs by
ROMIE FLANAGAN

Reading Consultant
LINDA CORNWELL
Learning Resource Consultant
Indiana Department of Education

CHILDREN'S PRESS® *A Division of Grolier Publishing*
New York • London • Hong Kong • Sydney • Danbury, Connecticut

Special thanks to the Koebels for allowing us to tell their story and for supplying the photos on pages 22 and 25.

Also thanks to the Michigan Farm Bureau for their help.

Visit Children's Press® on the Internet at:
http://publishing.grolier.com

Author's Note:
The Koebels' last name is pronounced KEE-bull.

Library of Congress Cataloging-in-Publication Data
Flanagan, Alice K.
    Raising cows on the Koebels' farm / written by Alice K. Flanagan ; photographs by Romie Flanagan.
        p. cm. — (Our neighborhood)
    Summary: Provides a basic introduction to the workings of a dairy farm, describing the feeding, cleaning, milking, and taking care of the cows.
    ISBN 0-516-21133-1 (lib.bdg.)   0-516-26470-2 (pbk.)
    1. Dairy farming—Juvenile literature. 2. Holstein-Friesian cattle—Juvenile literature. [1. Dairy farming. 2. Cows.] I. Flanagan, Romie, ill. II. Title. III. Series: Our neighborhood (New York, N.Y.)
SF239.5.F58 1999
636.2'34—dc21   98-7483
                                                                 CIP
                                                                 AC

Photographs ©: Romie Flanagan

Meet Mr. and Mrs. Koebel and their three daughters, Greta, Ava, and Tera.

The Koebels live on a large farm in Michigan. The farm has been in the Koebel family for a long time.

On their farm, the Koebels breed
Holstein cows. Holsteins are the
largest of all milk cows.

When cows breed, it means that a
bull and a cow have a baby. The bull
is the father.

The cow is the mother.

And the baby is called a calf.

A cow begins to give milk
after she has a calf.

8

The Koebels milk her
and sell the milk.

Mr. Koebel is in charge of the cows, or the herd. He is called the herdsman.

He feeds, breeds, cleans, and milks
the herd.

When Mr. Koebel is not with the herd, he is fixing farm machinery . . .

. . . or planting and harvesting the crops that the herd eats.

The Koebels grow alfalfa hay, field
corn, and soybeans.

They mix the crops and feed them
to the herd four times a day.

Mrs. Koebel takes care of the calves. She feeds them, cleans their pens, and checks on them often.

She also keeps all the records for the herd.

When Greta, Ava, and Tera are not in school, they help their mother.

18

They feed each calf milk from a bottle until it is about two months old.

At 6 o'clock each morning and
6 o'clock each night, the Koebels
milk the cows.

First, they wash each cow's teats so the milk will be clean. Then they attach the four teats to a machine.

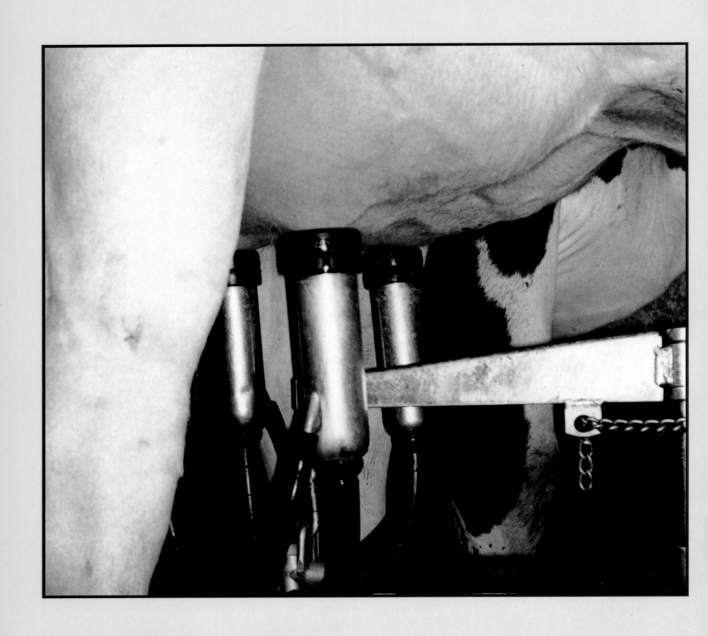

The machine gently squeezes out the warm milk from the cow's udder and sends it to a cooling tank.

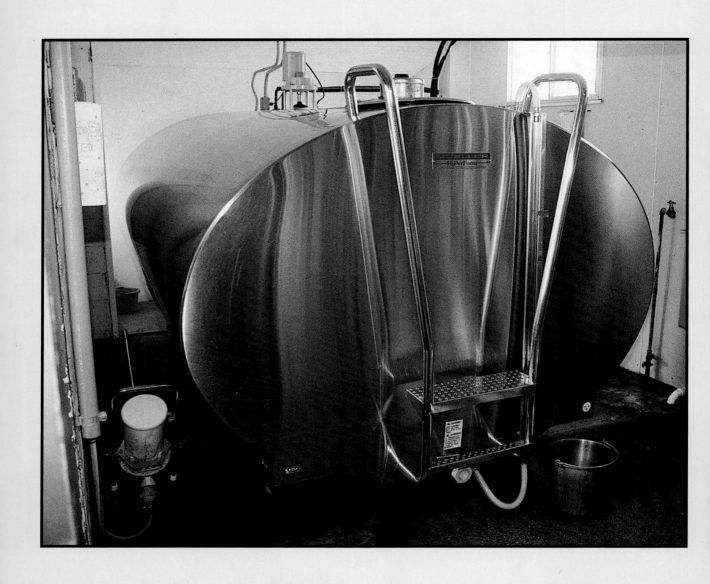

The tank keeps the milk cold until a truck takes it to a factory. There, workers get the milk ready for people to drink.

Today, Grandfather Koebel (on the left) makes sure that the milk gets picked up.

A computer keeps track of how much milk each cow gives and what she should eat.

At a feeding stall, the computer reads the number around each cow's neck.

It gives the cow the food she needs.

The Koebels take good care of the animals they breed.

They know that if they take good care
of their cows, the cows will give more
milk, the cows will have more babies,
and the cows will live a long time.

Meet the Author
and the Photographer

Alice and Romie Flanagan live in Chicago, Illinois, and have been involved in publishing for many years. Alice is a writer, and Romie is a photographer. As husband and wife, they enjoy working together closely. They hope their books help children learn about the people in their community and how their jobs affect the neighborhood.